DIRT SIMPLE

HAMMERED DULCIMER

BY Mark Alan Wade, DMA

National Hammered Dulcimer Champion

Online Audio   www.melbay.com/30361BCDEB

Audio Contents

1	Boil dem Cabbage	17	Liberty Reel
2	London Bridge Is Falling Down	18	Old Joe Clark
3	Shortenin' Bread	19	Chanter's Tune
4	Soldier's Joy	20	The Girl I Left Behind Me
5	Cripple Creek	21	Gallopede
6	Cincinnati Hornpipe	22	Stone's Rag
7	Golden Slippers in Upper D	23	Cold Frosty Morning
8	Golden Slippers in Middle D	24	Come Thou Fount of Every Blessing
9	Spring, from Vivaldi's Four Seasons	25	Leather Britches
10	Woodchopper's Reel	26	Silver Spear
11	Amazing Grace	27	Arkansas Traveler
12	Angeline the Baker	28	Flop-Eared Mule
13	Redwing	29	Left Wing, from "WAY Over the Waterfall"
14	Midnight on the Water	30	Liberty, from "Grass Roots"
15	Bonaparte Crossing the Rhine	31	Chanter's Tune, from "WAY Over the Waterfall"
16	Boys of Bluehill	32	Leather Britches, "from "Grass Roots"

© 2013 BY MEL BAY PUBLICATIONS, INC.
ALL RIGHTS RESERVED. INTERNATIONAL COPYRIGHT SECURED. MADE AND PRINTED IN U.S.A.
No part of this publication may be reproduced in whole or in part, or stored in a retrieval system, or transmitted in any form
or by any means, electronic, mechanical, photocopy, recording, or otherwise, without written permission of the publisher.

Visit us on the Web at www.melbay.com — E-mail us at email@melbay.com

Table of Contents

Credits:

Edited by Cristina J. Wade, MA, BME

Recorded and Mastered at Earthwork Studio, Newark, OH
by Brandon Bankes.

Photography by Mark Alan Wade.

All compositions are public domain and
edited and arranged by Mark Alan Wade.

www.MarkAlanWade.com

The Anatomy of the Hammered Dulcimer

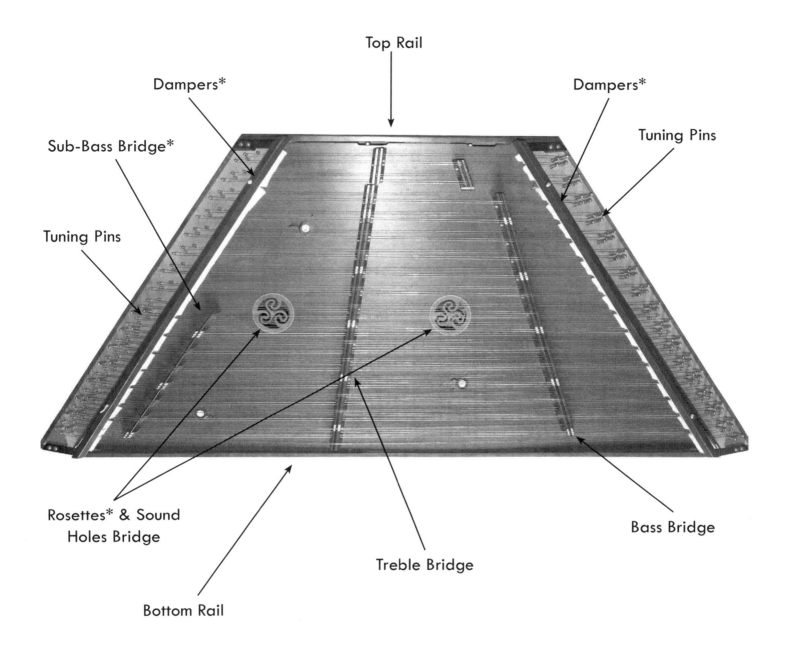

Top Rail

Dampers*

Dampers*

Sub-Bass Bridge*

Tuning Pins

Tuning Pins

Rosettes* & Sound
Holes Bridge

Bass Bridge

Treble Bridge

Bottom Rail

This dulcimer is a ~Cloud Nine~ 17/16/8 made by Michael C. Allen, Ostrander, Ohio,
with dampers and triple-spiral rosettes in the sound holes.
*Denotes optional features.

Accessories

Dulcimer Stands

There are several options for dulcimer stands. The most common is called a "Scissor Stand" because of the way it folds. This is a fairly light option and many cases have a spot for it right in the case. The downside to this type is that they are not adjustable.

Fully adjustable stands are great because they can be raised and lowered for standing or sitting. In addition, the angle can be adjusted to suit you. Unfortunately, these are much more expensive, heavier, and are not quite tall enough for me at 5' 10" to stand comfortably to play.

Scissor Stand

Adjustable Stand

I prefer the Tri-stander™ made by Dusty Strings. It is fully adjustable so you can even play on a hillside! The aluminum legs and mounting brackets are very light and the legs are telescopic, taking up very little room. There are three mounting brackets that are screwed to the bottom of the instrument and the legs screw off to store in your case. The drawbacks to these are their exorbitant cost at around $325 plus shipping and their industrial look. They are also easily stripped if you over-tighten them- a mistake that will cost you $205!

Tri-Stander

Tuning Accessories and Hammers

You will need an electronic tuner. There is no need to over-spend on this item, as there are many inexpensive options available. I use a tuner application on

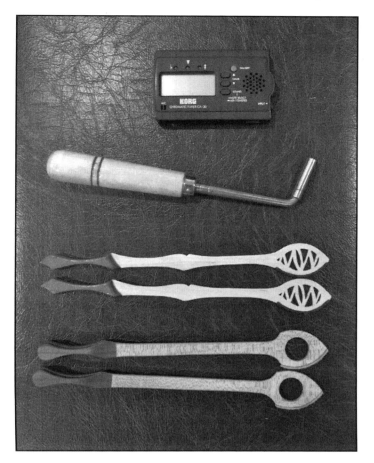

my iPhone for most tuning and it is incredibly accurate. When tuning for a concert or in other noisy venues when the tuner cannot "hear" my instrument, I use Korg CA-30 ($30) because I can plug my dulcimer's pick-ups directly into the tuner. This allows my tuner to give accurate readings even when I can't hear it myself. You can buy a clip or input to do the same for around $15. Then, to actually tune the instrument, you will of course need a tuning wrench. One should come with your instrument. I prefer the gooseneck style shown below because the added length gives you more fine control. The other popular option is a T-shaped wrench. Because your hand is right over the fulcrum point with this style, I find that you have less leverage, making fine adjustments more difficult.

Hammers

Look for two-sided hammers with a two-finger grip. That means there is leather on one side and wood on the other and the grip is wide enough to take two fingers on the bottom and your thumb on top. I much prefer the sound of dense maple to any other wood. Nothing comes close in my opinion. Ebony, for example, looks beautiful, but is too dense and causes a harsh and brittle sound. For beginners, I would select a length that is at least 8.25" long. My hammers are 9 1/4" long. In my almost 25 years' teaching experience, hammers shorter than 8 1/4" may result in the student using too much wrist and elbow motion to compensate for a lack of balance that is achieved with ample length. Flexible hammers sounds great too, but not for beginners. They require a firmer hand and are hard to come by.

Replacement Strings and Kit

It is a good idea to have a replacement string kit. All you need are needle-nose pliers, wire cutters (some pliers do this too), a CD storage case and strings. You can usually order a replacement string kit from your dulcimer builder. If not, you can use the stringing chart that comes with new instruments to order the number of strings in each gauge from a larger string manufacturer. I use the CD case to easily sort and stow each string gauge. The string envelopes fit perfectly into the CD slots and still allow you to easily see the gauge marking.

Finally, I keep all my hammers and tuning wrench in a hammer bag. You can buy one at any dulcimer festival for around $25. The one shown below is made by Crafts by Shannon and has my name embroidered on one side and my dog, The Beast, on the other. Her hammer bags and matching dulcimer dust covers are available on www.markalanwade.com. Dust covers allow you to keep your dulcimer out all the time without collecting dust and getting tan lines on your instrument. That's right! Your dulcimer is photosensitive too and leaving it out all the time can create "tan" lines.

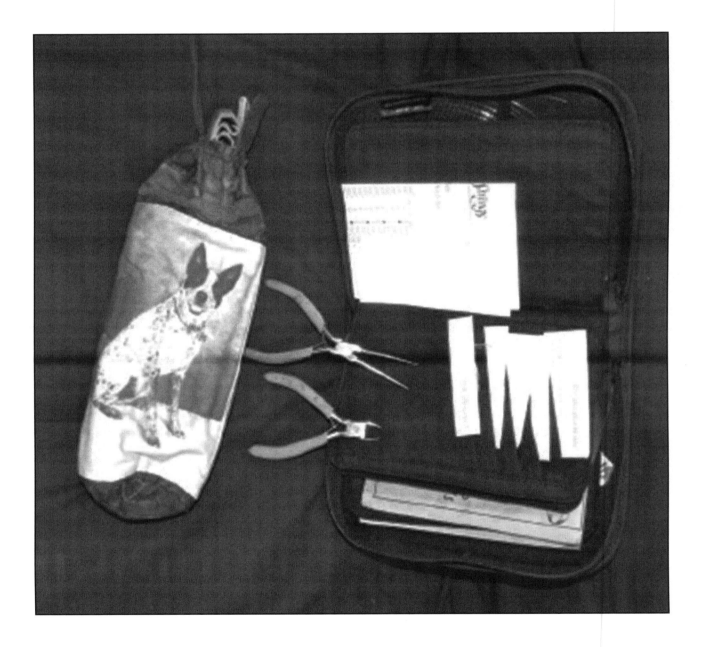

Tuning Your Dulcimer

It doesn't matter if you tune one bridge first or tune going up a bridge or down- just tune it! This is the single most important skill in dulcimer playing because if you can't play in tune, every note you play is wrong!

To Begin - Turn your tuner on and set it on the strings or wedge it in between courses (the pair of strings for each note) so you can read the dial easier. Always ensure that your tuner is calibrated to A=440 (standard pitch). The calibration function on tuners is only used when trying to tune to anything other than standard pitch. For instance, if you want to play with the piano at your church and the piano hasn't been tuned since 1970 and is around A=420. If that is the case, your 440 tuner would show that the piano is flat so you would calibrate it down until it registers in tune. Take a random sampling of pitches in differing ranges on the piano to get an average out-of-tuneness to calibrate. Then you can tune your dulcimer using your calibrated tuner and match it. For everything else- use 440!

To Tune: To put it simply - if a string is too high, loosen it; if it is too low, tighten it. Pluck an individual string and the tuner will show if it is sharp (too high) or flat (too low). If it is too high, turn your wrench counterclockwise to lessen the string tension; if it is sharp, turn it clockwise to raise the string tension.

Important: You will rarely **ever** need to turn your wrench more than 5 degrees unless restringing. Doing so is an easy way break strings or go so far that you end up tuning it to the wrong note entirely.

Tip: It is important to mute the other string in that same course because it will begin vibrating sympathetically and fool your tuner. In other words, there are two strings for every note. While tuning one string, the other will begin to spontaneously sound as well because it vibrates at the same frequency. When the string you are not tuning is left to vibrate sympathetically, your tuner will not be very accurate because it picks up both strings instead of the one you are actively trying to tune.

To Mute The Other String: I do this with my plucking hand at the same time as plucking the string to be tuned. While you pluck the string to be tuned with your index finger, use your remaining fingers of the same hand to touch the other string for that course to mute it.

It is critical that you get each string exactly in tune, as there are two strings involved for each note. If one string is only 2 cents flat (most people cannot hear this) and the other is two cents sharp, there will be a 4-cent gap between them that you **will** definitely hear.

Tip: only move the tuning wrench when the string is sounding. If you continue tuning after the string stops, you will not be able to gauge how far to tune.

Treble Trouble:
The treble bridge is hard to tune because you have to get both sides in tune and higher notes require even more finesse. As a rule, tune the side of your treble bridge that is opposite the side that your tuning wrench is on, e.g., if your wrench is on the left side of the dulcimer, tune the right side of the treble bridge first. The strings have about 16lbs of pressure on them at the bridge caps and this pressure will help hold it in tune while you fine-tune the other side. Thus, tune the side opposite the tuning wrench first, then, without moving the tuning wrench, fine-tune the same string on the other side of the bridge. It should be very close. This will ensure that the string will be in tune on both sides of the bridge.

The Seesaw Effect:
Just like children of unequal size seesawing, the strings on the upper side of the treble bridge may not have equal tension from left to right. Occasionally you will need to manually press down on the strings for fine-tuning. For example, if the left side is sharp and the right side is flat, press down on the string on the sharp left side to pull the pitch up on the flat right side. Then tune the left side with that slack now taken out. Just like if I seesaw with my three-year-old and he's stuck high up in the air, he will need someone to push down on his side which will in turn raise my side for us to be even. This tuning technique is a little advanced and can be intimidating. Ask your teacher or an experienced player for a demonstration.

Final Tuning Tips
- Check that your tuner is at 440Hz.

- Sharp means too high, so turn back counterclockwise.

- Flat means too low, so turn clockwise.

- Do not turn too far in either direction. Only tiny adjustments.

- Aim for perfection!

- Don't tune if you can't hear it yourself.

- Higher pitches have shorter wavelengths so you need to resound the string more frequently for the tuner to pick it up.

- If you are having trouble getting the notes of the treble bridge in tune on both sides, get the side of the bridge tuned that is opposite of the tuning wrench first; then fine tune the other side. If this doesn't work, press down on the strings to bend and pull any slack to the side of the bridge with the tuning wrench and take it out there.

How to Care For Your Dulcimer

- Do not leave your dulcimer where you wouldn't leave a child.
  - o Not in hot cars in the summer and not in cold cars in the winter.
- Leave it out as a part of your living space so you are more inclined to play it. Just don't leave it over heat registers, air-conditioning vents, or in front of windows. The vents can alter the humidity and (obviously) the temperature and could cause cracks. The sunlight will cause tan lines on your instrument, as wood is photosensitive.
- Do not be tempted by using strips of paper with the note names on them that you slide under the strings next to the bridges. These train your eyes to look at the wrong thing and prevent you from learning the note names. Instead, memorize the notes on your dulcimer without them and train your eyes to look at the bridge markers- NOT the strings. Also, your instrument will get tan lines if you leave the strips on there.
- Keep your home's humidity around 55% in the winter to avoid cracks. Use a violin humidifier inside your sound holes if you cannot control the humidity.
- Wipe down the strings with a soft dry cloth after you have touched the strings with your hands and fingers to make the strings last longer.

Replacing Strings

When to Replace Them
It's time to replace strings when they break or when they go false. A false string has corrosion on the strings from the humidity in the air and the salty acids on our hands. This causes the string to have an inconsistent diameter throughout and therefore the string has unnaturally occurring nodal points that reflect out of tune overtones. When you hear a string vibrate, you are actually hearing the fundamental tone (that you tune it to) and a rainbow of higher overtones that color the sound. False strings may tune the fundamental pitch okay but still sound bad to our ears because the overtones are out of tune due to corrosion. For lower strings that are wound, oils from our skin will build up over time and cause dust particles to collect in the tiny windings in addition to corrosion. The result is the same- a dead sounding string. If the string sounds dead with no ring or sounds out of tune- even when the fundamental is in tune with the tuner- it is time to replace the string.

How to Replace Strings
You will need the following: needle-nose pliers, wire snips, strings, the string gauge chart from your builder, tuning wrench and a tuner.
Step One: Remove the old string
Step Two: Unscrew the tuning peg so you have room to tighten the new string.

Step Three: Check your string gauge chart that came with your instrument for the correct gauge string. Then feed it through the bridges, anchoring the loop end on the non-moveable hitch pin.

Step Four: Thread the other end through the eye of the tuning peg and cut it off about an inch and a half past the tuning pin.

Step Five: Bend the end of the string back to about 45 degrees using your pliers. This keeps it from slipping out of the peg.

Step Six: Keeping the loop end tight on the opposite end, begin winding the string so that the windings wind tightly together below the eyehole of the tuning peg. You will need to guide the windings a bit as you go. There is an art to this! If in doubt about which direction to turn the wrench, look at the other strings for comparison. Do not bring up to pitch yet.

Step Seven: Once you have enough tension to keep the string on without holding it, check that the loop end is securely fixed all the way snug at the bottom of the hitch pin. They may ride up if too loose while winding.

Step Eight: Slowly bring the string up to pitch. With wound strings, gently lift up the string over the bridge cap to release tension every quarter turn. Some dulcimers will have a lot of pressure there and the string windings may catch on the delrin (the dense plastic rod on top of bridges) bridge tops, causing the string to break at that point. Lifting the string there allows the windings to slip over top and equalize the tension.

Stand Height and Angle

You should be able to reach most notes from a neutral position without changing your neck angle or back. In the illustration below, the player is in a neutral position. Notice how the back and neck of the player are constant for the low range, shown with the arms in solid lines, and for the upper range, shown in dotted lines. This is made possible by an ergonomic dulcimer height and angle that brings the instrument to YOU, NOT YOU to the instrument. If your dulcimer is too low or flat, you must compensate with your neck and back. If it is too high, you will feel it in your shoulders. In general, the more strings per course on your dulcimer, e.g., my 20/19/9, the steeper the angle will be in order to bring those notes to you.

PRO TIP: When we play in the high range, it is natural to move our bodies forward. Do so with your whole body, not from the waist up. In fact, stand with your left foot slightly in front of your right foot like a left-handed sword fighter. This will support you because when we do need to move up, it is up and to the left. Likewise, when we need to move back for lower notes, it is usually back and to the right. This is also how violinists support themselves with their instrument and left arm out in front. Your back and neck will thank you! Works when sitting too!

Hammer Grip

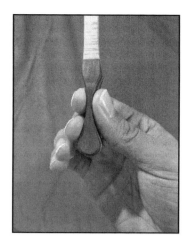

Active Grip

For all-around playing, keep those middle fingers in contact with the hammer! Also called the "Two-Finger Grip," the index finger and the middle finger hold the bottom of the hammer (hence, "two-finger") and the thumb is on top. This is an active grip because the fingers of the grip themselves produce the motion. In this hold, the index finger is the fulcrum and the middle finger is like a trigger to initiate the strike. The continuing motion comes from your fingers offsetting the weight of the hammer heads and the rebound from the strings–not from your elbow. The middle finger is partnered with the thumb in springing back against the hammer motion and redirecting it to the next strike.

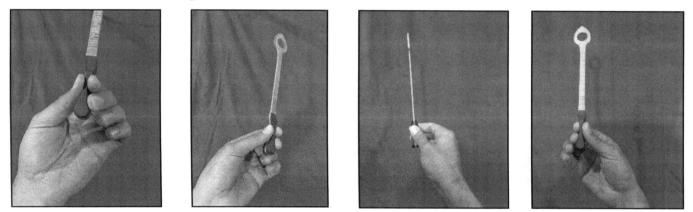

Passive Grip

Many great players use the passive grip successfully as their main grip. In my teaching and playing experience, this grip produces less accuracy and is less efficient. This is a "one-finger" grip as only the index finger is on the bottom and the thumb is on top. It is a passive hold because the motion originates in the elbow and pronation of the forearm rather than in the fingertips. The hammer subsequently flops as a result. I do use this grip when performing multiple bounce strokes and other rudiments because it facilitates the redirection of the rebound strokes.

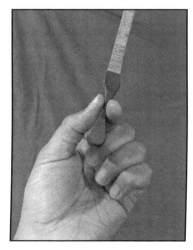
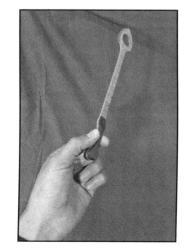
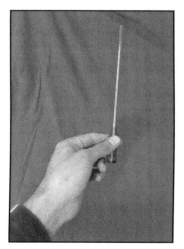

Ready to Play!

Finding the notes on your dulcimer is easy! Dulcimers are tuned in scale boxes where all the notes of a scale are grouped together, unlike on a piano where you need to know which black and white keys to use.

Imaginary Scale Boxes

Scales can be found on your dulcimer by starting on a bridge marker and going up 5 strings if you are right-handed (or 4 if you are left-handed) and finishing up to the left. For example, for a D scale, you will start on D on the right side of the treble bridge and play D, E, F#, G, A (if you are right handed). If you are left-handed, you will only play: D, E, F#, G. This difference is to keep you from crossing your hands. Then, you will move to the left side of the bridge to finish the scale with: B, C#, D (for right-handed players), or A, B, C#, D (for left-handed players). See the illustrations on the following page.

You may not have noticed that the scale boxes create an interesting pattern of scale keys. Starting at the top of the treble bridge, the 1st scale box has no sharps or flats- that's C major. The 2nd box just below has one sharp (F#), or G major. Below that is two sharps- D major; and below that is A major with three sharps. You will notice that each scale box shares notes with the adjacent boxes. I used the left-handed version of the scale to make it easier to recognize the pattern. The same is true on the bass bridge (the right bridge). Scales beginning on the bass bridge have their top halves on the right side of the treble bridge. The illustration below only shows the boxes on the treble bridge to avoid the clutter of seeing all eight together. The middle C box has no sharps or flats; the box above has one flat (F major); the box below has one sharp (G major); and the lowest box has two sharps (D major).

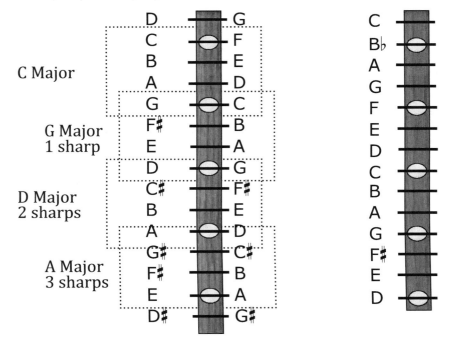

Finding the Notes in the Key of D

Since most dulcimer tunes are in D, let's start there. As you can see, there are two D Scale Boxes- one low and one in the mid-range. Most fiddle tunes are played in the mid-range so we'll focus our attention there. The low D scale is usually written in Bass Clef because those notes lay beneath the treble staff's range. Notice that each box contains two "A"s. Right handed players will use the "A"s on the right, and left-handed players will use the one on the left (you should alternate hands). You can also see that the notes of the D scale continue up on the upper left side of the treble bridge. Most fiddle

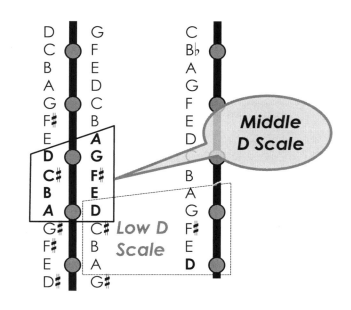

tunes will continue up there too. The only note above D on the treble bridge that isn't in the key of D is the high C natural. Chromatic dulcimers will have this C♯ somewhere added at the top.

Below is the enlarged treble bridge D Scale with the hammer patterns for left- and right-handed players, and all the notes numbered. Practice playing the scale up and back down.

Righties

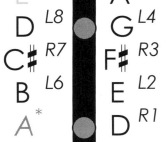

*This A is for left-handed players.

Lefties

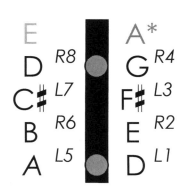

*This A is for right-handed players.

Finding Note Names On Paper

After you can find the notes of the D Scale on your instrument going up and down the scale, always alternating hands as you go, you are ready to learn how these notes are written in music. This mid-range D scale is written using the treble clef shown here: 𝄞. There are five lines and six spaces around them. To indicate which pitch the music calls for, a note head (the round part) is placed either on a line or on a space. The stem of a note tells you the note's rhythm. If you start on an A and go up, it's just the alphabet. Every letter will alternate being on a line or a space. It's simple! Since music isn't written alphabetically though, these mnemonic devices may help.

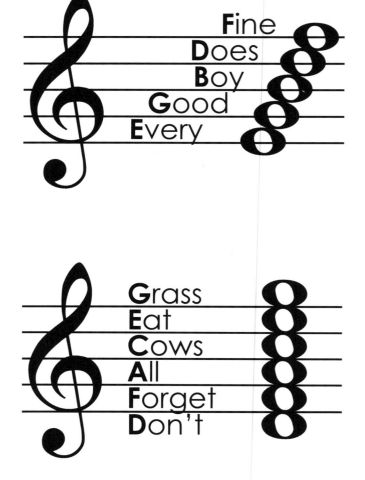

Notes on Lines
The line notes, from the bottom up are: E, G, B, D, F. You may remember this from grade school:
"Every Good Boy Does Fine."

Notes on Spaces
The notes on the spaces between, above and below the lines are are: D, F, A, C, E, G. You can come up with your own mnemonic device to remember these, but I use:
"Don't Forget All Cows Eat Grass!"

Try quizzing yourself on these note names. You can make or buy flashcards for easy review. In no time, you will have these memorized! It is definitely worth the time and effort to memorize them! Learn all the line notes, all the space notes, and then mix them up. Try writing them yourself! Spell words like: cab, bag, deaf, cabbage, fad, cage, and more!

Finding The Note Names On Your Dulcimer

The notes of the treble clef are easy to find on the dulcimer. The space notes begin with D. That D matches up perfectly with the dulcimer's D on the marker, found on the right side of the treble bridge. The line notes begin on the E above that marker on the treble bridge and the other lines notes continue up the right side of the treble bridge.

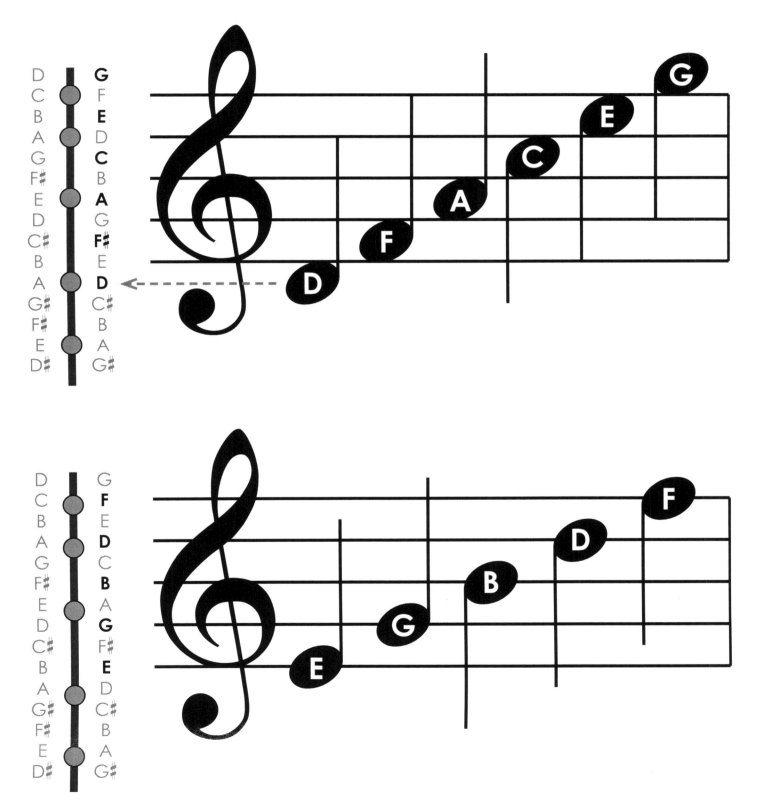

17

Activity:
- Try playing the line notes on your dulcimer: E, G, B, D, F- All on the right treble bridge. Say them aloud as you play them.
- Play the space notes on your dulcimer while saying them aloud: D, F, A, C, E, G.

That still leaves a lot of strings on the dulcimer to find in music notation, but this will get you started. The first songs we will cover will be in the Key of D and in the "D Box." The illustrations above are great for the right side of the bridge and include the 1st 6 notes of the D scale: D E F♯ G A [B] (normally B is played on the other side of the bridge.) When the music gets to the 3rd line of the staff, the middle line, you will typically switch to playing those notes on the left side of the treble bridge as shown in the D box. In fact, most notes on the dulcimer are found in multiple locations and the player chooses which one to strike based on what key the song is in and which hand will hit it. To keep this Dirt Simple, for now, we'll stay in our D box.

Review: D Scale Box and Its Notation

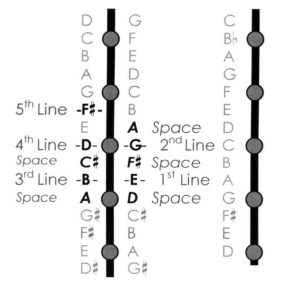

The notes of the D scale use the bottom 4 lines in music notation on the treble clef, as in: "Every Good Boy Does." It also uses the spaces on the staff from the D below the staff, found on the marker. This illustration also shows two A strings - one on the right treble bridge for righties and one on the left treble bridge for lefties.

Activity:
- Now find these 5 line notes (E, G, B, D, F(♯)) INSIDE your D Scale Box as shown above. This means that you will now play D and high F♯ on the LEFT side of the treble bridge. Notice that the top line F♯ goes beyond the scale box.

- Find the space notes (D, F(♯), A C(♯)) INSIDE the D Scale Box too. D, F and A will be the same as the illustration on page 18 on the right treble bridge. To stay in our D scale box and ensure that Cs and Fs are sharp (♯), you will play the C(♯), E and G space notes on the left treble bridge. The illustration above only goes as high as the C♯ space note because E and G go above the D scale. Even though the D scale stops at the note D, it's good to know those notes as well.

Rhythm Notation Explained

There are two parts to every written note. The note heads, as explained in the previous pages, show the pitch of the notes. The note STEMS or lack thereof indicate note durations, or their rhythm. Notes can have stems alone or stems with flags or beams. Notes without stems indicate rhythm too, but this is also specified by note heads that are not filled in solid. It's really not as complicated as it may first appear.

Note Durations

Note durations are all based on a given note's proportion to the entire measure. A measure is a group of beats in recurring patterns, the most common of which is four beats in a measure. In fact, this is called common time. The note durations are all based on common time. Measures are determined by the regularly occurring groups of stressed and unstressed notes. In common time, also notated as 4/4, the pattern is: Strong beat one, weak beat 2, Less Strong beat 3, weakest beat 4. This is more important to the music writer than for the music reader.

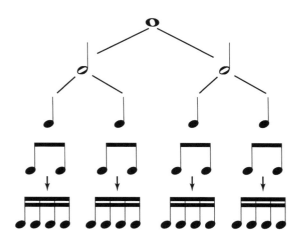

Whole Note = a whole measure, 4 beats

Half Note = half a measure, 2 beats

Quarter Note = 1/4 of a measure, 1 beat

Eighth Note = 1/8 measure, 1/2 beat

Sixteenth Note = 1/16 measure, 1/4 beat

Other Notation

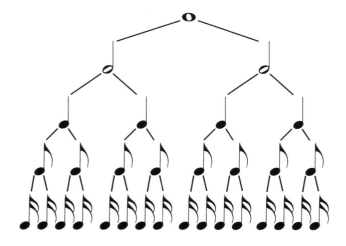

When 8th notes and 16th notes occur singularly, they are notated with flags instead of beams. As you can see from this illustration, the use of flags causes visual clutter. It is much more common to see these notes beamed instead.

Rests

For every note value, there is an equivalent symbol for that duration of silence, or a rest. The chart below compares the notation of notes with their corresponding rests. In most fiddle tunes you will not encounter rests but it is important to recognize them when they do arise.

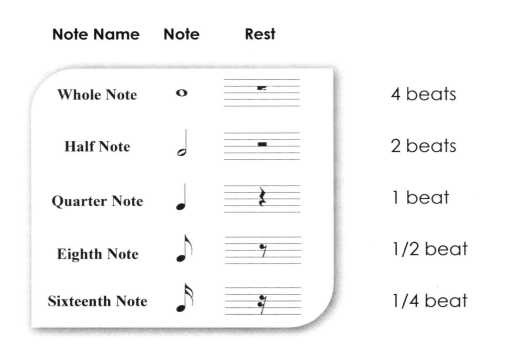

Note Name	Note	Rest	
Whole Note			4 beats
Half Note			2 beats
Quarter Note			1 beat
Eighth Note			1/2 beat
Sixteenth Note			1/4 beat

Counting Rhythms

Since music has meter (the recurring pattern of strong and weak beats) it is easy to count. You just number off those big beats every measure.

Each beat, 1 – 4, is called a downbeat. When there are two notes in the span of just one beat, or 8th notes, the first is called the downbeat and the 2nd is the up-beat. The downbeat will keep the number for the beat this occurs on and the weaker up-beat is counted as, "and."

For example, if you have quarter notes on beats 1 and 2, then two eighth notes on the third beat, and a quarter note on beat 4, you would count, "One Two (Three &) Four."

It is possible to say the right rhythm counts but with the wrong rhythm so make sure that you say "three &" on one beat in the same amount of time you say counts 1, 2, and 4. This is where your feet will keep your time accurate. Tap your foot while you say the counts, keeping your foot pulse steady.

More Examples:

These measures show eighth notes on different beats in each measure. Try playing these on your dulcimer- any string is fine. Tap your toe while you play!

16th Notes and Triplets

Often music is written with three or four subdivisions of a downbeat. When a beat contains three pulses, it is notated as a triplet, which looks like three beamed eighth notes, often with a bracket, and the number three to indicate that all three

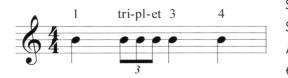

squeeze into one beat. When counting these, just say, "tri–poh -let", on the beat with the triplet. Avoid compressing the three notes and take the entire beat to evenly space the three pulses.

16th notes are used when four notes fit in the time of one beat. Notice that they have two beams. Just like in counting eighth note rhythms, the first note in the group of four that falls on a downbeat keeps the number of that beat in the measure. The remaining three micro-beats are counted as "e & a."

For example, "1 e & a" or "2 e & a."

Mixed Rhythms

Sometimes you will see a mix of 16th and 8th notes. As with other divided beats, the downbeats will keep the number of the beat. Count the other upbeats with their corresponding syllables.

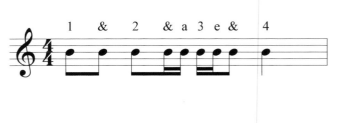

Dotted Notes

Sometimes a note will sustain for three beats. To total three beats, you would need a half note plus one more beat. This is notated as a dotted half note. By placing the dot beside the half note, the note gets the original value of two beats PLUS half of the value of that note. So two beats for the half note plus (half of a half note's 2 beats = 1 beat) for a total of three beats! Technically you can dot any note, adding half again the value of that note, but in traditional music you are not likely to run into this. Most likely you will just see this in waltzes, which have three beats in a measure.

Other Meters

All of the musical examples so far have been in the most common meter of 4/4. 4/4 is one example of a Time Signature that we use to indicate meters. There are a few others that will feel familiar in traditional music too. Waltzes have three beats (1 strong, 2 weak, 3 weakest). This meter is notated with the time signature 3/4. Polkas and some other fiddle tunes are written in 2/4, or two beats to a measure. The key to understanding time signatures is knowing what the top and bottom numbers mean in the signature. The top number tells how many beats in a measure. The bottom number indicates how those beats are notated. The bottom number "4" in all these examples means that the beats are quarter notes. In classical music, often the composer will chose to write music with half notes or eighth notes (or other!) representing the beats. In traditional music, you will almost always encounter 2/4, 3/4 or 4/4. The one exception you may see is 6/8, or Jigs. This meter is most often used in Irish music and is called a compound meter because the big beats are divided into threes. Specifically, 6/8 is a compound duple meter in that there are two BIG beats that are each subdivided into three micro-beats. If you were to count it out, you would have **ONE**, 2, 3 **FOUR**, 5, 6. Since jigs are fairly lively, it is usually too fast to be able to count out all 6 micro-beats, so we commonly count it as **One, Two**. Technically speaking, the two numbers that make up the time signatures in compound meters mean entirely different things than in simple meters like 2/4. When you are ready to tackle playing jigs and slip jigs, or if you enjoy music theory, you can read all about it!

22

Rhythm and Hammer Lead

It is impossible to talk about one without the other. These two hot topics are completely inseparable and can lead to disagreements between even the best of dulcimer friends! This issue is simply a question of which hand to lead with. Some propose that the dulcimer is a left-handed instrument because it gets higher as you go up and to the left and, therefore, everyone should play with left hand lead. Others propose that you should lead with your dominant hand and cite that some of the best players around are right-handed. And some say that you should just play everything as it comes with no hand leading at all.

What We Can Learn From Percussionists

After much study and almost 25 years of teaching, I defer to my percussion training- I am a college band director by day! Every beginning percussion book teaches right-hand lead from the very beginning. Right-hand lead is taught early on (even to lefties) because the height of the band experience for drummers is marching band and drum corps. Drum lines are judged on their visual appeal and having uniform sticking patterns not only causes the ensemble to sound the same but look the same too. Imagine a row of 12 drummers drumming with all the right hands and left hands synchronized- it's pretty fun to watch! Since most of the population is right-handed, the lefties conform to right-hand lead. For the righties, leading with the dominant hand feels natural and gives organic pulses and stresses where it rhythmically makes sense. Right-hand lead works for left-handed drummers just fine because there are no notes involved, just one big drumhead and the rim to strike. Alternate hand lead, however, is another system where the player alternates hands at will. It has two purposes- to eliminate any natural pulses that occur with dominant hand lead and, more importantly, to prepare the students to play mallet percussion. On the xylophone, for example, there is only one of each note and they only go left and right. Their bars do not to go out in front of them like a dulcimer and unlike the dulcimer, each pitch only happens in one place. Naturally, when only playing sideways, moving left and right, there will be a lot of hand crossing. To avoid tying mallets in knots, they are taught to not lead with any hand and to switch hands and double up as needed to avoid these crossings. Again, this only makes sense for this specific application.

What I Teach and Why: Dominant Hand Lead

I strongly believe that dulcimer players have the most success when they play with their dominant hand leading. We get the same benefit of having natural pulses and stresses fall on our dominant hand. This is also the default by human nature, as most of us would play with dominant hand lead anyway. Unlike the xylophone, the dulcimer has two or three of almost every single pitch. There is seldom reason to cross your hands. If choosing one placement of an A causes you to cross your hands, play that A or the note before or after in a different spot! 99% of hand crossings, particularly by righties, can be avoided by a better choice in placement of the note in question or the notes that precede or follow the problem spot. I very seldom make any exception to dominant hand lead and that is usually when playing Bach. There is no comparison to the rhythm, groove and fluency of dominant hand lead and absolutely no legitimate reason not to use dominant hand lead on an instrument that gives you 2 or 3 places to put each note!

I, myself, am left-handed but I have infinitely more experience teaching successful right-hand lead players. Since we lefties are substantially out-numbered, I use right-handed notation in the songs that follow. If you are also left-handed, simply do lefts for "R"s and rights for "L"s in the notation for the tunes that follow.

Dominant Hand Lead

Dominant Hand Lead simply means that your dominant hand plays the strong downbeats and your non-dominant hand plays the upbeats. It does not mean that your non-dominant hand should be weak! This point is where rhythm and hammer lead are married. Downbeats are the whole beat numbers 1-4.

Up-beats are the "ands" of the beat, or the 2nd half of the beat. When tapping your foot on the beats, these happen when your foot is off the ground. In 4/4 they are notated as 8th notes and they are the 2nd of each pair of eighth notes. The first measure below shows a measure with only downbeats. The second measure has all of the down beats with their up-beats. Notice that the numbered downbeats are all played with the dominant hand and the up-beats are played with the non-dominant hand. Try playing these examples on any two pitches.

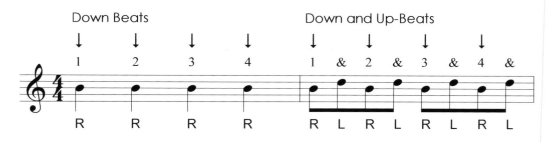

These examples show how to find down and up-beats when subdividing the beat in half. The illustration below shows that when a beat is divided into 4ths, e.g., 16th notes, 16th notes are counted as the beat number, which remains the downbeat, then "e & a."

In the previous example with 16th notes, the "ands" of the beats are also notated with down arrows. Their arrows are smaller to illustrate that in comparison to the weakest subdivisions, "e" and "a", the "&" of the beat feels stronger, but not as strong as the downbeat. In other words, 16th note subdivision is felt as: strong, weak, less strong, weakest for every beat. It is all relative. When the "&" of a beat occurs in the context of only quarter and 8th note rhythm, they are the weakest subdivision and played with the non-dominant hand. However, in tunes where running 16th notes are the norm, the "&" of the beat is played with the dominant hand- partly by feel, but more importantly, because you will have just played your non-dominant hand on the 2nd 16th note.

Practice Examples

In *Shave And A Hair Cut*, the smallest note value is an 8th note, so the downbeat of beat 2 (the first 8th note) is struck with the dominant hand, and the second 8th note (the up-beat) is played with the non-dominant hand.

Shave and a Hair Cut

The next example features mixed rhythms. The first measure uses only quarter notes and eighth notes and the second measure has 8th and 16th note subdivisions. When the 8th note is the smallest note value in the 1st measure, the downbeat is the dominant hand and the non-dominant hand gets the weaker up-beat. In the 2nd measure, the dominant hand starts every downbeat as usual. On the 3rd beat, the 16th notes are played RLRL and the 4th beat returns to eighth notes again.

Dotted Notes

Dotted notes can be tricky. The key is to hammer the rhythm as if ALL the subdivisions were there. In *Amazing Grace*, for example, the 9th measure contains a dotted quarter note on beat one. That means that the A string sustains for a beat and a half, or the downbeat of beat 1, its upbeat ("&"), and the downbeat of beat 2. The 1st note is a downbeat and played with the right hand as you would expect, but the "&" of beat two, the F♯, may pose a hammering question. The solution is to play that F♯ as if you played all the missing subdivisions before it. If you played, "1 & 2" before it, you would use "R L R." And since the F♯ is also the weak up-beat, it would be played with the non-dominant hand.

Amazing Grace

Angeline the Baker uses dotted 8th notes. The same principal applies. In the example below, the original notation is shown in the first measure and the counting rationale for the hammer patterns is in the second measure. Beat 2 is a dotted 8th note (it gets ¾ of the beat, or "2e&") followed by the "a" of beat 2. When in doubt, always hammer the rhythm as if all of the missing subdivisions that are tied up in the dotted note were there. IF you had a note to play for beat 2's dotted value, you would have, "2e&", played, R L R. That leaves the weak up-beat "a" to the non-dominant hand. I notated this in the 2nd measure by writing out 3 Ds to represent the dotted 8th note D in the original and marking the "e &" in italics as a reminder that they are not in the original. The answer is the same, dotted notes produce weak up-beats in 4/4 as a byproduct and a non-dominant hand almost always follows them.

In addition to the dotted 8th notes, this tune also uses syncopation by placing the strong melodic note D on a weak up-beat of beat 3. It may feel awkward to play that with the non-dominant hand, but it is correct.

Quick Tips To Easy Dominant Hand Lead

- When you encounter a rhythm with two beamed notes, the 1st of the two is always the dominant hand, and the 2nd is weaker and played with the non-dominant hand. This is true with 16th notes and 8th notes (and 32nd notes if you ever see them!).
- Many songs do not start on downbeats, or at least on beat 1. In these cases, the preemptive notes are called pick-up notes. If there are an even number of pick-up notes, start with your dominant hand. If there are an odd number, start with your non-dominant hand. This will allow you to land on your dominant hand for the downbeat of the first complete measure.
- In waltzes, even though there are an odd number of beats (3), there are an even number of subdivisions. Stick to dominant hand lead.
- Triplets: when you have an odd number of subdivisions you have a choice in hammer patterns. If you start the triplet on your dominant hand, you will end up on your non-dominant hand for the next downbeat. Either start the triplet with your non-dominant hand or double up your dominant hand to get back to dominant hand lead.
- All downbeats are played with the dominant hand.

Your First Notes!

In this first song you will find all of the notes on the right side of the treble bridge in the D Scale Box. Even so, it is important to learn to use dominant-hand lead. That means that each measure will start with your dominant hand. Also notice the sharps at the beginning. This is called a key signature and this indicates that the notes F and C will be sharp for the entire song because the song is in the key of D. If you stay in your D box, the Fs and Cs are already sharped for you.

Boil dem Cabbage 1

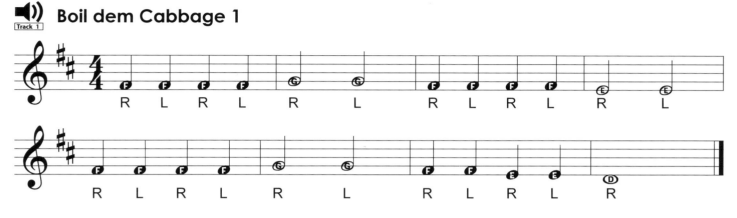

Style: Even though the melody above is the singable tune that matches the lyrics, this song is usually played with a bouncy swing rhythm that mimics the strum of a guitar. Below, the tune is notated with this strum-like rhythm that sounds like, "run horsey." This style adaptation also requires a closer look at dominant-hand lead.

Quick tip: When in doubt about your hands, the first note of a beamed pair will always be your dominant hand. Because the dominant hand lands on every downbeat, you will notice you will have two right hands in a row and the weaker up-beat (the 2nd note in the beamed pairs) gets the left hand.

Boil dem Cabbage 2

London Bridge Is Falling Down
Good Habit: play all Bs with the left hand on the left side & all the As on the right!

27

Crossing The Bridge: On certain slower songs, it is completely acceptable to double up your hammer patterns. In this song below, playing with strict dominant hand lead causes unnecessary hand crossings (but it's great for lefties like me!). For example, in right-hand lead, you would leave the 2nd note of the song with the left hand and have to cross your hands to get to the left side of the bridge for the B. Try this pattern instead!

🔊 Shortenin' Bread

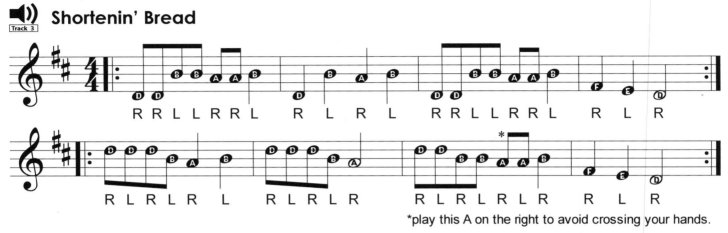

*play this A on the right to avoid crossing your hands.

Upper D Scale: The D scale continues up the left side of the bridge after D into another octave. This fiddle tune takes you up as far as high A.

Pick-Up Notes: Many songs do not start on beat one. The notes before the first downbeat are called pick-up notes. In this song, there is a quarter note B pick-up. Arrange the hammer pattern so that beat one lands on your dominant hand.

Repeats and Endings: Most fiddle tunes have 2 melodies- an A and a B part. Each part is repeated. Notice the double bars with a colon. These mean to repeat the previous section. On the 1st pass, play the measure under bracket 1. Skip that measure on the 2nd pass and jump to the 2nd ending.

🔊 Soldier's Joy

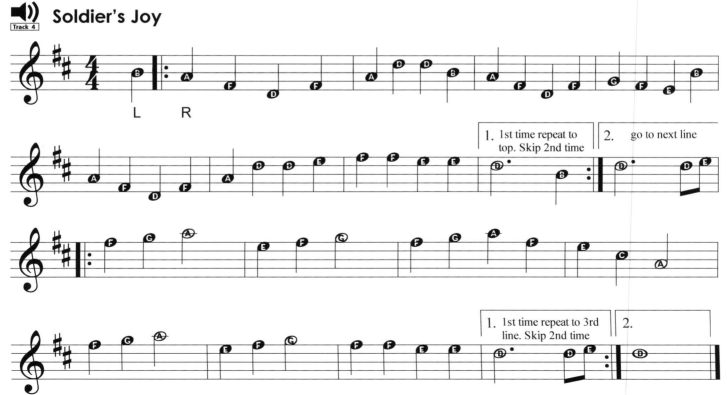

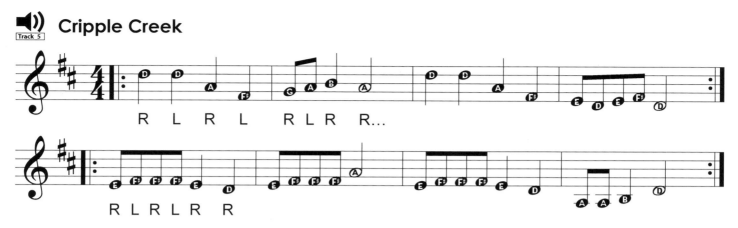

Now here is *Cripple Creek* with the traditional "run horsey" rhythm. Watch your hammer patterns for this style and follow dominant hand lead as always. Also notice that the B Part (the 2nd section) has a variation that goes down to low A, found on the bass bridge across from treble bridge E or below the D on the right side of the treble bridge. Remember- all downbeats get dominant hands. That means that the first note in each beamed pair of 8th notes is your dominant hand; the second will be your non-dominant hand.

Cripple Creek 2

Tips to Learning Tunes Faster

Recognizing Patterns

Fiddle tunes use patterns that make sense to our ears. They do this in several ways, like repeating phrases and using familiar scale patterns. In *Cripple Creek*, notice that the 1st and 3rd measures and the 5th and 7th measures are the same. This is because fiddle tunes use a question/answer format. Measure 1 asks a musical question and measure 2 finishes the question. Measure 3 reiterates the question before measure 4 gives a stronger answer. The same is true for the B part. That conversation in English would be something like: "How do you get to *Cripple Creek*?" "How do you get to *Cripple Creek*, you ask? It's at the end of this road." In the following tune, Cincinnati Hornpipe, measures 1 & 2 are the question phrase, measures 3 & 4 are the answer; measures 5 & 6 repeat the question, and measures 7 & 8 give a firmer answer. Cincinnati Hornpipe also uses scale patterns. For example, the notes in measure 2 all move stepwise around the

D scale, as does the pattern in measure 4, 6, and 12. Finally, the B part of this tune has a simple melody of E F♯ G F♯ - first it is presented with filler As in between, then in the 3rd measure of the B part, it is compacted to only one A note in between to build momentum before the snowballing descending scale.

🔊 Cincinnati Hornpipe
Track 6

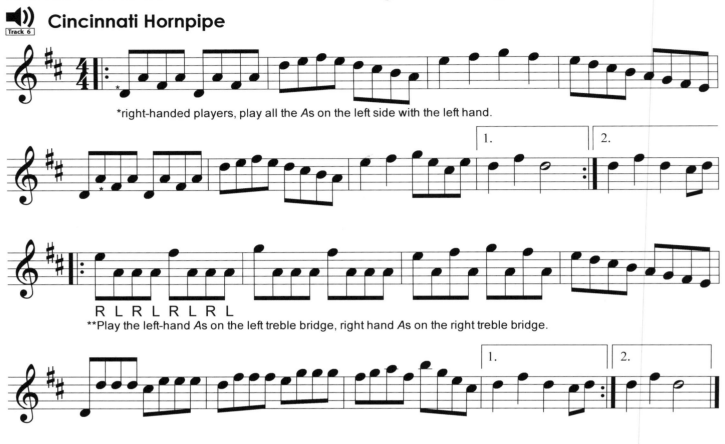

*right-handed players, play all the As on the left side with the left hand.

R L R L R L R L
**Play the left-hand As on the left treble bridge, right hand As on the right treble bridge.

Exploring the Upper D Scale

Golden Slippers falls between the D scales, using the top half of the middle D scale and the bottom half of the upper D scale. It is worth learning in at least two octaves for variety, but I'll first present it here in the upper D scale. On the music staff, this scale begins on the 4th line D. On your dulcimer, it is on the left side of the treble bridge.

Right Hand Right Side / Left Hand Left Side
This is one handy "rule" that is almost always applicable to keep your hands from crossing unnecessarily. The 5th and 6th notes of the scale always occur in two spots. In the D scale, A and B are found by continuing straight up from the 1st note of the scale AND they are found on the left side of the treble bridge. As a rule, play with dominant-hand lead. Then, when one of these notes falls on a RIGHT hand, play the string on the RIGHT side. When following sound dominant-hand lead, play the string on the LEFT when it falls on a LEFT hand. This will keep your hands from crossing and encourages us to cross the bridge to the left with the left hand and to cross to the right with the right hand.

Hand Independence

Some tunes sound incomplete without accompaniment. For classical pieces, unless you play in a group with arranged sheet music, you will need to play your own chords. There are two ways this is done: ostinatos and harmony. Spring, from Vivaldi's Four Seasons, features both techniques. In the A part, the right hand plays an ostinato (a repeated pattern) of D on the bass bridge and A on the right treble bridge. Notice that the ostinato is notated with note stems that point down and the melody's stems point up. First learn the melody in your left hand for the A part, and then practice the right hand ostinato alone. When you can do both easily on their own, start the right hand "motor" then take off with the melody. The B part utilizes parallel harmony in 3rds. Most players find this is easiest with the right hand on top because of the angle of the bridges and hammers – even lefties like me! The key to playing in parallel harmony is to set your eye on the hand with the melody. The other hand will learn to follow along in tandem. For more on these embellishment and self-accompanying tricks, check out my Mel Bay book, *Harmony Time for Hammered Dulcimer*.

Notes: This tune presents two rhythmic points for your attention. Watch out for the three dotted half notes and allot them all three beats. The other concern is the tied note in the penultimate bar. Sustain the E through the duration of the original quarter note AND the 8th note to which it is tied.

🔊 **Spring** From Vivaldi's Four Seasons
Track 9

32

Woodchopper's Reel is a perfect piece for learning D and A chords and practicing their arpeggios (chords played one note at a time). The melody itself is almost entirely composed of ascending and descending arpeggios. I have included their chord names above the notation to aid in identifying chord patterns. Explore using the Ds and As on the bass bridge and the treble bridge. See which you like best.

🔊 **Woodchopper's Reel**
Track 10

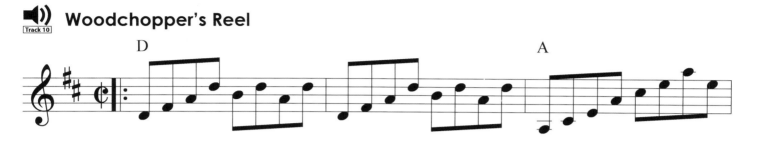

Pentatonic Scales

Pentatonic scales are simply five-note scales. They are commonly used in folk music in virtually every culture in the world. In fact, wind chimes are even tuned to pentatonic scales. Chances are that you have already heard a pentatonic scale today whether in a song, in the air or in someone's cell-phone ring. The reason that this scale is so popular is that there are no dissonant intervals- that is to say; there are no two notes in the pentatonic scale that do not sound good together. That is why the random collisions of wind chime bells are soothing. The pentatonic scale is a major scale with all of the dissonant half steps taken out. The 4th and 7th scale degrees (notes) of the major scale are omitted because there are half steps between the 3rd and 4th degrees (F♯ & G in the example below) and the 7th and 8th (C♯ and D). When these trouble-making intervals are removed, the resulting intervals are pleasing to the ear. That is why this scale is so useful in improvisational playing. You (almost) can't hit a wrong note if you stay in this scale! Here's how it works.

Scale Numbers:	1	2	3	4	5	6	7
Notes:	D	E	F♯	G	A	B	C♯
Solfège:	do	re	mi	fa	so	la	ti

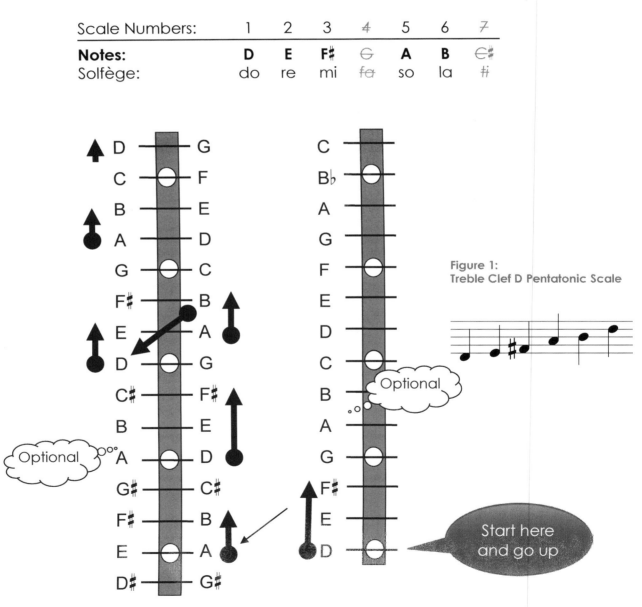

Figure 1:
Treble Clef D Pentatonic Scale

Optional

Optional

Start here and go up

Amazing Grace is the first pentatonic song we'll start with. This rendition places the melody in D pentatonic and it sits right between the low D and middle D scales. It's amazing indeed that this song only has 5 notes! One final observation: this song is in ¾. That means there are three beats in a measure. Interestingly, every phrase begins on a beat three, starting with the first pick-up quarter note on beat three and every phrase thereafter. Before you start, find these notes on your dulcimer and practice identifying them at sight on the sheet music.

🔊 Amazing Grace
Track 11

This next pentatonic tune is *Angeline the Baker*. This one is usually played an octave higher than *Amazing Grace*. The easiest way to play this is to play all notes on the left treble bridge.

🔊 Angeline the Baker
Track 12

35

This tune is not pentatonic but does sit between two D scales. Redwing was one of the first tunes I learned on the dulcimer and is great for learning rhythm. Here you will encounter dotted half notes (3 beats) and dotted quarter notes (1 ½ beats). The counts are written in to help you. The B part of the tune has long sustaining notes that require ties. A tied note means that the note sustains through the duration of the first note all the way through the value of the note it is tied to. This is notated with an arched line. The first occurrence is in the third measure of the B part. Traditionally dulcimer players and strummers alike will fill this long note value with "run horsey run" rhythm- especially instruments that do not sustain fully, like mountain dulcimers and mandolins. To hear what this tune is fully capable of, check out my recording from my *Way Over The Waterfall* CD, included as BONUS TRACK #29 on the CD for this book, where we play it as a lullaby, old-time, ragtime, boogie-woogie and rock-a-billy!

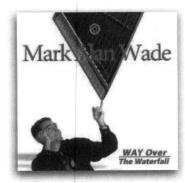

◀) Redwing
Track 13

This great waltz has some tricky rhythms that will feel very intuitive after listening to the recording. In addition to dotted notes, this song also has syncopation and a triplet. Syncopation is when a note is accented on an upbeat, like in measure 3. The 2nd note of the bar is an A that is a strong melodic note on the upbeat of 1 with sustain via a tie. I wrote out the counts so that you can learn to count similar rhythms in the future when a recording is not available. Lastly, there is a triplet on beat 3 of measure 7. Just squeeze all three notes into the space of that beat and use the word "tri-poh-let" itself to help you hear how it fits.

Midnight On The Water

Track 14

Here is a fun march that is very easy to learn. Since this tune feels more like it is in 2 beats a measure than 4, I wrote it in cut time. That only means that you will tap your foot twice a measure. You can also think of it in a fast 4/4. Now that you have some practice with the right-hand/right side rule, I will begin abbreviating this as LTB for left treble bridge and RTB for right treble bridge. Generally speaking, this will also indicate which hand you should use: left for LTB, right for RTB.

🔊 Bonaparte Crossing the Rhine

Hornpipes

Hornpipes are a style of tunes that accompany a dance by the same name. Characteristically, they are played with a heavy long-short swing to the 8th notes. They also have a trademark "stomp, stomp, stomp" (3 quarter notes) in their phrase endings. Compare the endings of The Cincinnati Hornpipe with Boys of Bluehill and you will recognize this common feature. Even though it is not in the title, *The Boys of Bluehill* is a hornpipe indeed!

🔊 **Boys of Bluehill**
Track 16

R   L   R L R L R   R L   R L R L R L   R   L

R   R L   R   R L

Here is one of the first fiddle tunes I learned many years ago: Liberty Reel. We gave this tune a fun newgrass feel on my CD, Grass Roots, included as BONUS TRACK #30 on the CD for this book. Liberty is a perfect tune for mastering the D arpeggio. Arpeggio means a chord played one note at a time in succession; literally, "harp-like" in Italian. The B part features the D arpeggio in its 2nd and 4th measures.

Tips: Watch out for the triplets in the endings. I suggest starting the triplets on the dominant hand and using the 2nd quarter note that follows to get back to dominant hand lead as shown below.

🔊 **Liberty Reel**
Track 17

New Note: C♮

So far all of the tunes in this book have been in D major. This next song is in neither D major or minor. It is in a new modal scale called Mixolydian. Scales that do not conform to the major or minor patterns of whole and half steps are called modal. Mixolydian is most similar to the D major scale except it calls for C natural instead of C#. C Natural is a pitch that you will usually encounter in other scales because the key of D major uses C#. I usually play this scale entirely on the right side of the treble bridge. *Old Joe Clark* uses 3rd space C and middle C (which is notated with a ledger line because it is lower than the lowest note on the treble clef. Middle C is only found on the bass bridge. Below is the D Mixolydian Scale.

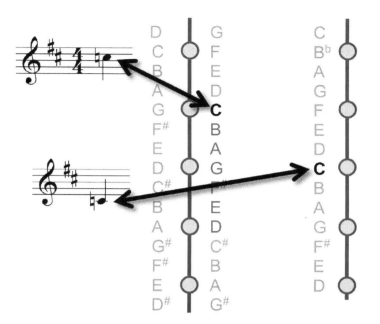

D Mixolydian

🔊 **Old Joe Clark**
Track 18

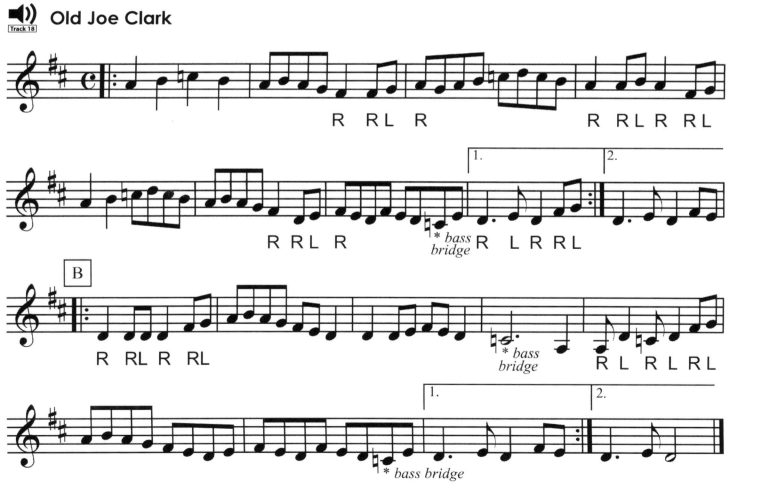

The mode or key of some tunes can be ambiguous, like this great polka, *Chanter's Tune*. The key signature implies that it is in the key of G, however, it is decidedly D-centric. If you scan through it, you will also notice that despite the F♯ in the key signature, there are no Fs in the melody at all. Verdict: the tune is in D Mixolydian just like *Old Joe Clark*. It is played from D to D using all the notes of G major and has the characteristic lowered 7th note, C natural. The F♯ in the key signature implies that the harmony chords will be D major. Finally, this tune is a polka because it is an Irish tune in 2/4. For a wild interpretation of this funky tune, check out my recording of it on my CD, *Way Over The Waterfall* , included here as a BONUS TRACK, #31 on the CD!

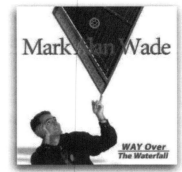

Tip: You may find it easier to play the low Ds on the bass bridge. Be sure to start each beamed pair of 16th notes with your dominant hand.

🔊 **Chanter's Tune**

Track 19

42

Tunes in the Key of G

The introduction of the note C natural is a great way to begin learning songs in G. The G major scale is simply the next scale box higher than D.

G Major Scale Box

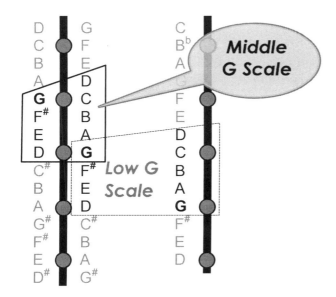

Common G Major Pitfalls:
In the key of D, the note C is sharped by the key signature so you probably don't think about it. In the key of G, when you read the note C, remember that it is C natural and stay inside your G scale box! The key of G has only one sharp and that is for F♯.

🔊 **The Girl I Left Behind Me**
Track 20

43

Right Hand / Right Side Rule Review

The 5th and 6th notes of Major scales are found in two places on the dulcimer. In the key of G, these notes are D and E. They are found on the RTB by continuing straight up from the G scale box: G A B C D E – all on the right. They are also found on the LTB, directly across from G and A. When one of these notes falls on a right hand when playing in correct dominant-hand lead, play that D or E on the RTB. When it falls on a left hand, play it on the LTB. This next tune is a great study piece for this important rule. Notice that there are 2 Ds in a row between the 2nd and 3rd measures of the third line of this piece. The first D is an up-beat and played with the left hand on the left side. The 2nd D falls on a downbeat in the dominant hand. Since the right hand plays this one, play it on the RTB. This will ensure that you never have to cross your hammers or deviate from dominant hand lead.

🔊 Gallopede
Track 21

Syncopation

Rags are usually full of syncopation; that's what makes them sound "ragged."
Stone's Rag achieves this with the use of ties. Remember the tie and dotted note
"rule": these rhythms almost always will call for the non-dominant hand to follow.
In the first and subsequent measures below, for example, the 1st note after the
tie will be an upbeat with the non-dominant hand. Also be ready for the C♯ that
comes up from time to time.

Stone's Rag
Track 22

2nd time, skip to 2nd ending.

Play B if your dulci-
mer has no D♯

Cold Frosty Morning is another modal tune, like *Old Joe Clark*; it isn't major or minor. This tune is in A Dorian and shares all the same notes and key signature with G major, but it is A-centric. The A Dorian scale is: A B C D E F♯ G A. In other words, it is a G scale that goes from A to A instead of from G to G.

The triplet in the second measure is going to require some hand choreography. As discussed earlier, you can either start the triplet with the non-dominant hand so that the next down beat will land on your dominant hand OR double up your dominant hand with two in a row to get back to dominant hand lead. Since the preceding note is a quarter note and you have some time, I would recommend starting the triplet with the non-dominant hand.

🔊 **Cold Frosty Morning**

Track 23

I put my spin on one of my favorite hymns by playing it in the additive meter, 3/4 + 4/4. That means that there is a regularly occurring pattern of a measure of ¾ followed by a measure of 4/4. It sounds perfectly natural and is not nearly as hard as it might look on paper. This hymn is featured on my CD, *Grass Roots*.

Track 24 **Come Thou Fount of Every Blessing**

This is a very popular tune among contest fiddlers that I chose as the finale to my CD, *Grass Roots*, included as BONUS TRACK #32 on the CD for this book. I learned this rendition years ago and it is quite different than what I hear fiddlers play. My version also has a C part that you probably won't hear anywhere else. Enjoy!

 **Leather Britches**

Notation Versus Tradition

Many Irish tunes have ornamentation written in like the turns in Silver Spear below. By tradition, the turn is actually played in the manner shown in the second "Interpretation" version. You may also see the rhythm of the turn notated as a triplet, but if you do your homework and study recordings, you will hear that triplets in Irish reels are almost always played as two 16th notes and an 8th note.

Silver Spear

Interpretation

49

Repetition

When a musical pattern of notes repeats itself, it is called a Sequence. Most tunes have sequences, but the example in *Arkansas Traveler* is very easy to see. The third measure of the B part presents a sequence repeated three times. This pattern consists of three downward steps following by a leap back up to the starting note. This four note pattern is then repeated a step lower each time. Recognizing patterns like this quickly will make you a faster sight-reader and help you learn the tune faster.

Patterns are the result of repetition. Notice that the first and second endings are nearly identical. In fact, they only differ in their final pick up notes, depending on where they send the music, i.e., back to the A part or to the B part.

Tip: In the endings, begin on the left treble bridge and wait to cross over to the right treble bridge until the D on the right side with the right hand. Right side – right hand!

On the CD that accompanies this book, you will notice that this song makes excellent use of dampers. Dampers have felts that absorb the string vibrations when the player steps on the pedal, causing very short note lengths.

🔊 **Arkansas Traveler**
Track 27

Some fiddle tunes are in two different keys- one for the A part and one for the B part. This makes them even more fun to play and hear, but can cause confusion when it is time to stop. Stopping on the B part feels strange because it's not the home key you started in. In this case, the A part in is the key of G and the B part is in the key of D. Usually, tunes like Flop-Eared Mule will end after a repeat of an A part. In a jam, someone will usually indicate this by raising their foot or shouting out, "Last time!" after playing the songs several times and during the last time through an A part.

Flop-Eared Mule

Track 28

Glossary

Active Grip
A hammer hold in which the fingers themselves produce the motion.

Additive Meter
One definition of this tune that is exemplified in this book is a time signature that consists of two regularly repeating smaller time signatures. Example: 3/4 + 4/4. A piece using this meter would have a measure of 3/4 followed by a measure of 4/4 throughout.

Alternate Hand Lead
A system of hammering in which the hands alternate, regardless of rhythm.

Arpeggio
The rendering of a chord one note at a time in succession. Literally, "harp-like" in Italian.

Course
A set of two (sometimes three) strings tuned to the same pitch and struck together on a hammered dulcimer. The strings are places approximately an 1/8 inch apart.

Dominant Hand Lead
A system of hammering in which the dominant hand plays the dominant, strong beats. Strong beats include all downbeats and the first of any pair of beamed notes. The non-dominant hand plays the upbeats. This is the preferred method of hammering and produces an unparalleled rhythmic accuracy and flow.

Dorian Mode
A tonality and scale that is easiest to conceive of by envisioning it as a major scale that is played from Re to Re, e.g., re mi fa so la ti do re. Example: E Dorian uses the identical notes of D major, but is played from E to E: E F♯ G A B C♯ D E. Another way to think of it is a minor scale with a raised 6th note.

Downbeat
Notes placed on whole numbered beats: 1, 2, 3, 4. These beats have more weight and are named from the human nature of tapping our foot down on these strong beats.

Hornpipe
A traditional dance tune that features a heavy swing to the 8th notes and typically features three quarter notes in the endings.

Key Signature
The sharps and flats added at the beginning of a song and every line of music thereafter indicating the notes to be sharped (raised) or flatted (lowered) throughout. This indicates to the performer which key (scale box) they will play in.

Ledger Lines
When a pitch lies above or below the range of the staff lines, a separate line or multiple lines will be written on a note-by-note basis to show how much above or below the staff a given pitch is. For example, middle C is written in treble clef below the staff with a single line through the note head.

Mixolydian Mode
A tonality and scale that is most like a scale that spans from the fifth note of a major scale to the fifth note an octave higher. For example, D Mixolydian uses all the notes of G major (D is the 5th note of G Major) but is played from D to D inside the G box. Another way to think of it is a Major scale with a lowered 7th note.

Mode
A tonality of melodies and 7-note scales other than major and minor that are often used in traditional music.

Ostinato
A repeated pattern of notes used as an accompaniment. From the Italian for obstinate.

Passive Grip

A hammer hold in which the motion originates in the elbows, wrist and pronation of the forearm, causing the hammer to move sympathetically.

Pentatonic Scales

A five-note scale that is most similar to a major scale without the 4th and 7th notes.

Polka

A fiddle tune form in 2/4 whose form is AABB.

Rag, Ragtime

A musical style that, in fiddle tunes, is swung and features syncopation.

Reel

A fiddle tune form in 4/4 whose form is AABB.

Sequence

A repeated pattern of pitches. Example: 1231, 2342, 3453, or ABCA, BCDB, CDEC

Staff

The five lines onto which musical notation is written.

Syncopation

A rhythmic term for strong melodic pulses on typically weak beats.

Time Signatures: simple meter and compound meter

This is a pair of numbers placed in the first measure of the music that indicates how the beats are arranged and counted. In simple meters, the top number indicates the number of beats per measure and the bottom number indicates which note value is used for the beat. In 4/4, there are four beats in a measure; the quarter note, represented by the lower "4", indicates that the beat is notated as a quarter note. 3/4 means there are three beats in a measure and that the beats are written as quarter notes. 2/2 (synonymous with cut-time used in Bonaparte Crosses the Rhine) means there are two beats in a measure and the half note (represented by the bottom number "2") gets the beat. In compound meters, the beats are divided into 3 subdivisions. In this type of meter, commonly used in Jigs, the top number is the number of subdivisions of the beat and the bottom number indicates the note value for the subdivision. For example, 6/8 (a jig) has six subdivisions of the beat and those subdivisions are notated as 8th notes. The "big" downbeats in 6/8 that are each divided in threes are notated as dotted quarter notes as this note value is worth three 8th notes.

Treble Clef

The symbol written at the beginning of the staff to indicate that the notation will be for notes above D4. Any notes below that, for example, middle C, will use ledger lines.

Turn

An ornament that instructs the player to play the: written note, the note above, the written note, the note below and the written note in quick succession in the amount of time of the note value of the note above which the symbol is placed. In traditional Irish music, this symbol is played at two 16ths and an 8th note for the given pitch.

Up-Beat

Named from the location of our foot when tapping to a beat, up-beats are weak beats when your foot is off the ground. Practically speaking, these are the "ands" of beats, or the 2nd half of beats that follow downbeats.

Waltz

A tune in triple meter indicated most often in folk music with a time signature of 3/4.

Alphabetical Index of Tunes
* indicates songs that have been recorded on Mark's CDs.

Recordings by Mark Alan Wade

Grass Roots – "I began playing the hammered dulcimer in 1989 and the first songs I learned were traditional fiddle tunes. This is my 7th CD and I am more excited than ever to return to the roots of my dulcimer journey with over twenty years of playing behind me. You will hear influences from the various stops along my dulcimer journey: Classical precision, wild Bluegrass improvisation, progressive New-grass arrangements, and Irish waltzes."

The core of this CD is the *Mark Alan Wade Trio*, comprised of Denison University music faculty members: Andy Carlson (fiddle, mandolin), Casey Cook (guitar) and Mark Wade (hammered dulcimer). Available on iTunes or on my website.

Just As I Am – Mark's second album presents traditional country hymns drawn from diverse musical influences–from blues to classical. This recording features the hammered dulcimer accompanied by varied instruments, including: guitar, bass, mandolin, flute, percussion, fiddle, and vocals on three tracks. Besides Just As I Am, the CD includes: *Wayfaring Stranger, How Great Thou Art, Ave Maria, Simple Gifts, The Sweetest Gift* and many more.

WAY Over the Waterfall – *WAY Over the Waterfall* takes traditional tunes to a new dimension of artistry with jazzy improvisations and tasty embellishments. Featured on this CD is Alex De Pue, 1999 National Fiddle Champion (Winfield, Kansas), Mark Kreis and other great musicians. This CD features great arrangements of: *Billy Bob's Blackberry Blossom Boogie (Blackberry Blossom), Lime Green Sleeves (Greensleeves), Wrongs of Man (Rights of Man), Danny Boyz (Danny Boy), Flight of the Bumble Bee-Bop* and many more.

Silver Bells – *Silver Bells* is a delightful Christmas album filled with instrumental arrangements of holiday favorites. So original! So different! So beautiful! Mark is again accompanied by 1999 Winfield Fiddle Champ, Alex De Pue who frequents the stage of the Grand Old Opry. You will want to play this CD year-round. Includes *Silver Bells, Sleigh Ride, What Child Is This?, Canon in D, Joy to the World, O Holy Night, Winter Wonderland, Silent Night* and other Christmas favorites.

Hammer On! – Mark's ensemble project, *Hammer On!* consists of four multi-instrumentalists – all four play the guitar – all four play the hammered dulcimer – the possibilities are endless! Mark is joined by Dan Landrum, Yanni's renowned hammered dulcimer player, Randy Clepper on cittern, guitar, hammered dulcimer and tenor banjo, and Bob McMurray on guitar and hammered dulcimer. Hammer On! music is loaded with an arsenal of driving rhythms and hot licks. Includes: *Rondo in 7/8, Enamored, Cluck Old Hen, Falling Water, En Gedi, Sweet Georgia Brown* and others.

Serenade – Romantic classical pieces and timeless ballads on solo hammered dulcimer. Tracks include: Chopin's Nocturne, *Op.9, no.3, Clair de lune* by Debussy, *Prelude from Cello Suite, No.1* by J.S. Bach, *Smoke Gets In Your Eyes, The Swan* by St. Saëns, Schubert's *Ave Maria, Largo* by Rodrigo, *A Time for Us* (theme from Romeo and Juliet) and many more.

Books

Tunes & Techniques for Hammered Dulcimer – 120 pages. For absolute beginner through Advanced. A Must Have for serious students! 60 pages of techniques and illustrations; 60 pages of music to play! There is an optional 80 min. CD.

15 Minutes a Day – A daily technique routine book for catapulting your playing to the next level. Assumes you know chords and scales.

Easy Does It! Popular Jam Tunes – This innovative book presents a treasury of fiddle tunes that you should know in two ways- an easy version and a standard version. This way the book is great for beginners through players who want to grow to be able to play it like I do.

Harmony Time: Embellishments for Hammered Dulcimer – This entire book is dedicated to answering the question: "How do I add accompaniment and embellishments to melodies on the dulcimer?" It illustrates how to enhance great tunes to showcase their inherent musicality. Full of illustrations, preparatory exercises and easy-to-play arrangements, Harmony Time comes complete with audio CD for aural learners!

Killer Technique for Hammered Dulcimer – This is a concise method book for refining your dulcimer technique and removing the road blocks in your playing that are holding you back. Lots of illustrations and easy-to-play exercises!

www.MarkAlanWade.com

About the Author

National Dulcimer Champion, Mark Alan Wade performs in orchestra halls and music festivals alike with his characteristic mix of classical precision and raw traditional American style. Classically trained as a trumpeter with doctorate and master's degrees in music from The Ohio State University, his unique style emerged as the technique and discipline of his formal training crossed over into his dulcimer playing. He earned his undergraduate degree in music at Ohio Wesleyan University. His performances bring world music to life and revitalize familiar classical pieces on hammered dulcimer.

Mark Alan Wade is based in Northeast Ohio, but his 25+ years performing have taken him all over the U.S., Europe and Asia. In 2013, he was a featured performer and lecturer at the World Cymbalom Congress in Taipei, Taiwan. 2014 found him playing trumpet in an orchestra on the very stages where Beethoven and Haydn performed near Vienna, Austria. Recently he premiered his Irish hymn suite for hammered dulcimer and orchestra, "Streams of Mercy," with the Tuscarawas Philharmonic Orchestra. His upcoming touring schedule includes performances in Los Angeles, Chicago, Orlando, London (U.K.), and Albuquerque. Wade has also performed with the Beach Boys, the Buckinghams, and with numerous orchestras including the Columbus Symphony Orchestra, Mansfield Symphony, Springfield Symphony, Tuscarawas Philharmonic Orchestra, Lima Symphony, Newark-Granville Symphony, and the West Virginia Symphony Orchestra.

Despite his active performing schedule, he maintains a thriving private studio with six of his students having also won the National Contest for hammered dulcimer. He has held a professorship in trumpet, hammered dulcimer, music theory, and wind ensemble at Denison University.

He has published seven hammered dulcimer CD albums, including *Serenade*, a collection of classical gems for hammered dulcimer. More information can be found at: **MarkAlanWade.com**

Other Mel Bay Hammered Dulcimer Books

Harmony Time: Embellishments for Hammered Dulcimer (Wade)

First Lessons Hammered Dulcimer (Thomas)

Hammered Dulcimer for the Young Beginner (MacNeil)

Getting Into Hammered Dulcimer (Thomas)

Killer Technique: Hammered Dulcimer (Wade)

The Hammered Dulcimer (Hughes)

The Hammered Dulcimer's Companion (Mason)

You Can Teach Yourself Hammered Dulcimer (MacNeil)

A Collection of Original Music for Hammered Dulcimer and Other Instruments (Rizzetta)

A Scottish Christmas for Hammered Dulcimer (Sansone)

An Old English Christmas for Hammered Dulcimer (Thomas)

Ancient Noels (Sansone)

Bluegrass on Hammered Dulcimer (Page)

Celtic Fair (Sansone)

Celtic Meditations (Sansone)

Easy Does It! Popular Jam Tunes You Can Play for Hammered Dulcimer (Wade)

Hammered Dulcimer Arrangements for Special Occasions (Carter)

Hammered Dulcimer Classics (Koenig)

Hammered Fiddle Tunes (Thum)

Maggie's Big Book of Celtic Tunes (Sansone)

Middle Eastern Music for Hammered Dulcimer (Justice)

Scottish Songbook for Hammered Dulcimer (Page)

Shall We Gather: Hymns for Hammered Dulcimer (MacNeil)

Sounds of the Season (Sansone)

The Hammered Dulcimer Treasury of Tunes (Hawley)

The Sandbridge Dance Tune Collection: Arrangements of Reels, Jigs, Hornpipes, Polkas and Rags for the Hammered Dulcimer (Kolodner)

The Sandbridge Waltz and Slow Air Collection: Arranged for the Hammered Dulcimer (Kolodner)

Tis the Season (Page)

With This Ring: A Hammered Dulcimer Collection for Weddings and Special Occasions (Page)

Windrift (Sansone)

Arranging for Hammered Dulcimer (Page)

Hammered Dulcimer Chords (Page)

WWW.MELBAY.COM

WWW.MELBAY.COM